73

The Cardboard Sublime

છ

poems by Oliver Sedano-Jones

Write Bloody UK

www.writebloodyuk.co.uk

First edition.
ISBN: 978-1-8380332-4-8

Cover Design by Angelo Maneage
Interior Layout by Winona León
Edited by Fern Beattie
Proofread by Fern Beattie
Author Photo by Emmanuel Blessed

Type set in Bergamo.

Write Bloody UK
London, UK

Support Independent Presses
writebloodyuk.co.uk

The Cardboard Sublime

THE CARDBOARD SUBLIME

it is your love / must feed the dancing snow
– Ted Berrigan

with the mask of behaviour I do not protect
my raw genuine self – I overcome it
– Susan Sontag

To You in the Future:

The sun explodes; we're one grilled cheese.
I keep chewing the cud of each day.

Flavour: mum holding dad's hands until he stops.

When I was young I thought I'd one day see
into people's hearts like display cabinets.

Lesson: don't be young.

We held hands and watched him twist
like a sprig of burning parsley.

Yes.
Sorry, I meant: No.

PART 1.

WE KEEP TALKING BUT ALL I HEAR IS A POWERING DOWN ENGINE SOUND LIKE A CAR CLUTCH-CONTROLLING ITSELF OFF A CLIFF

What's the point in being perfectly compatible
      if one of y'all's too freaky to show off at parties.

                      What's the point – tax breaks?
A child's fist curling softly in the moon. A skeleton with dexterous hands self-throbs
      the ice cubes in its ribs.

Was eating a burger when the patty grew wings and flew into the sun.
                      Years later a telegram:
    You were an inattentive lover and an indifferent BBQ attendant, farewell.

Today I set my Word proofing language to *sound and fury, signifying nothing* (UK).

Everything that has happened, happened
      for a reason says my doctor and that reason was Dick Cheney.

The idea that people should be making more people. Don't Make People.

      I've never read Frankenstein but my understanding
is that it concerns an upwardly mobile med student
      who resents his baby's effect on his career.

      Why didn't you take my pain into account before adding me
to your list of disappointing passions? Asks

my pet koala. I don't even know
      what this has to do with marriage anymore,

but since I met you I've pronounced it *mar – hee – ahj*, with a swish
                  of horsehair perfume.

I'd kiss you says my therapist but I find you loathsomely unattractive.
      I'd kiss you says my priest but I serve a jealous master.

What is a man? A miserable pile of secrets, says Dracula

                then we fight

Burning Elephant

Last night I read 'Meditations in an Emergency' by Frank O'Hara
Then I read 'Mirror Traps' by Hera Lindsay Bird

Then I read 'The Glass Essay' by Anne Carson
Then I read '[Trying to see the proportional relation]' by Ariana Reines

Then I read 'Why I Left You' by Selima Hill
Then I read 'Meditations in an Emergency' by Frank O'Hara again

In short, I read all the poems you sent me
Thinking I'd write you one in return

I wanted my poem to be about coming to terms
With food or time or parents or something

But I couldn't sustain the conceit
Because strawberries were raining all over

The patio again big red sweet dollops
And I found myself writing about how

My love for you was a burning elephant
Which was very embarrassing

Because my love for you is actually more like
A petite-but-deadly slasher film antagonist

Or a cavernous stadium where twenty-two
Footballs kick around a tiny footballer

Or a lion who lives in the stem of a tornado
Flying his heart round and round on a string

As a child I didn't act out much and I regret it
I didn't dye my hair or flirt with my teachers

I didn't cut myself or steal my parents' prescriptions
I rebelled in silent ways, with my thoughts

Loving you has been an opportunity to misbehave
Loving you has been a chance to indulge this feeling I've always had

I miss you like Kim misses Kanye
I miss you like Neruda misses being alive

Every time the sun eats another night
I want you to choke me with your thin warm hands

I want you to choke me with your thin
Simulation of affection

Sorry to go on like this
It's just you were perfect in every way

Horses were leaping through French windows
I was eating mangoes straight off the tree

Now you crop up between everything
Like a bitter cactus

I lie in a heap thinking about you
Good heavens [...] I'm just like a pile of leaves

Did I mention I stopped eating recently?

SOLITUDE
after Ella Wheeler Wilcox

Lately I've found myself laughing at jokes that aren't funny
I can't help it – laughter leaps out of me like a meat cleaver
slashing at my grim facades of appropriate adult behaviour
the sad old earth must borrow its mirth

Serious art gets better reception and wins more prizes
violence and injustice, epiphany, grief
action movies are popular because destruction is popular
like a thirsty plant that spams kaboom flowers
but when things go bad my first instinct is to snort and cover my lips
when you insult me I feel it wriggling on my face like a worm's
        tunnelling-scar
and when I split open again with the lung shudders oh
how we laugh, the whole world with me

Sing, and the hills will answer
I sing and am often lauded for it: "shut the fuck up" screams
        everyone, delighted
but sometimes you have to bite the bullet and say the things everyone
        wants to hear:
jazz pavlova, honey carousel, marble pigeon, murder hammock
swan grenadier, Kentucky Fried Anarchy, Frankenstein Sinatra Jr
The Fast and the Spurious 2: (Too Fast, Too Spurious)

Rejoice, and men will seek you / but I'm not seeking men: as they're raining,
        it's unnecessary
unless you mean my repressed inner man-child that is
in which case yes I find myself rejoicing as I red-rover
the gestapo circling my heart, to quote Kevin Barnes
who my friends describe as "fey" and "a narcissistic little bitch"
which is just plain old homophobia even if true

Bitch and the world bitches with you, defend on principle and you defend
        on principle alone
is my motto, whenever anyone tries telling me O'Hara's not the best poet
        of '57 after Milosz

I hear a fulsome whistle blowing: it's the foghorn on Vin Diesel's spurious
    monster truck
he's racing the horsemen of the apocalypse, who are experts of the genre
always waiting until the last second to feed their horses the nitro pellets
but it's my Jungian anima that roars into flame
each time I leave you dissolving in tasteless mood lighting

There is room in the halls of pleasure
it's a nostalgia banquet back at mine:
The Mask dispensing orange juice from his bullet holes
Keanu shushing those bullets as he stands to give a speech
I sit at his feet like a child and I don't know what it is that creeps
over my lips, or the nature of the moisture on my face

LOATHING

My inner child is in a hostage situation.
LOOK WHAT YOU MADE ME DO
I weep at him, hurling miniature
vodka bottles at the hotel mirror.
O, no! Alas, I rather hate myself
for hateful deeds committed by myself
cries the child, which is so precocious
it temporarily stems my wrath.
It's never the child's fault   oh no never.
Balloon strings jerked from the hand,
snails exploded aggressively underfoot,
hamsters were hugged to conclusion.
Inexplicable fire flowed into a petunia,
a garden frog, a marriage. Two young
lovers in the family photograph:
they too, were ruined. My outer child
is now demanding a bigger ransom.
Hotel mirror very drunk and threatening.
Decisions, decisions. Can I set fire to my ashes?
I want to dream I was always old.

POEM

As always, thoughts barged around in my head
like slug removal men casing a flower pasture.

You arrived to the funeral dressed in nothing
but scandalous renaissance heavenswear
and the dim furnace of your overachieving eyes.

I arrived in my pyjamas – not the fashionable ones –
and my feelings were also not fashionable. Wait, I pleaded,
but already you were folding away your gaze,
souring on us like a suitcase of earthy tapioca.

"Reaching out, I could not grasp even half your shadow"
was the turn of phrase that passed through my brain at the time.

You were gone, I was forced to think about things.
Think and eat canapés. Why leave me?

Thoughts surged in my head like slot machine iconography.
It was time to pull the little plastic lever at last.

To Be in Love With the Greatest Love Poet in History

would be excellent motivation
for writing a truly great love poem   you
     probably aren't
the greatest love poet in history   thank you
     for that

           just think:
if you were
the GLP   it would be impossible
       to tell you   that being with you
is like lunging   into a *red, red*
wood chipper full of macramé roses   for fear
     of straying into cliché

I couldn't tell you   your eyes
are two gold chainsaws
ripping through unicorn meat   in paradise

         and I'd be doubly ashamed
informing you that love
is a white tree   printed on the heart
by a beautiful bureaucrat   whose mouth is heaven
     or that a kiss
from you makes gemstones
pour from my nostrils   and the quantity
       is just enough
to buy sexual and spiritual redemption forever

I'd be afraid, you see   of seeming infantile and ridiculous
     to a writer
of such sublime insight and quixotic skill   whose highly original take
on the whole romantic weltschmerz

had guided generation after generation   into the maelstrom
          of annihilating epiphany   time and time again:
          daisies, spring and harvest moons
growth and red things and fantastic arterial gore   if you were
          the GLP

I'd be feeling so much regret right now
          having failed to address the dilemmas
inherent   in ten thousand years
          of one-sided eulogy

problems precipitated   by the very fact
of your greatness   your knack
          your flair
the indescribable   flower
of your talent rising   in flames
on the page   love's passionate
resistance to definition   matched perfectly
          by the passionate eloquence   of the poem
that I failed to write

                              if you were
the greatest love poet in history   I would look
at your beautiful love poems
          then look at you
                    and you would be so ugly by comparison
but of course
you are the opposite of ugly   thank you
          for not writing those poems
                    moonbeams kiss the sea
                    at every pore with instant fires

wherefore art thou
          you are the sun

END OF THE TABLE

I am failing at life; I feel it in the back of my sputtering steam-brain
where I'm forever shovelling slick hunks of dream to keep it running.
I have tried to be reasonable in my expectations of myself
but whether I meet them or fall halfway into an interpretive dance about bees,
still they rise about me in a giant wave of sarcastic teenage peonies.
I had a pet once, it was a tortoise. It would very slowly move – crawl, I guess –
from one end of the table to the other. *Has it given up?* I'd think each time
it stopped, but no, tortoises NEVER give up. It would reach the end of the table
and I would feed it a leaf then lock myself in my room and cry.
How come I can never reach the end of the fucking table?

ALCATRAZ

you are pouring candy down my neck
remember
when i told you not to pour candy down my neck?

i take it back

fill my chest with shining wrappers

here is the first cat
to learn the piano, the first human
to armwrestle the fates

a first time to tell you how i feel

a knight surrenders his head to his liege:
cylindrical, like a can of corned heart-muscle

it rolls across the regal carpet, for your honour

it's a chiming deathlessness
debussy bells in a mirrored box
vampires waltzing in a UV disco

what a feeling sings the beautiful television

it's a mushroom cloud of moths
and fruiting spores of the moon
elements of a hex, the first non-wizard hex,

which does nothing, because how you are
is fine with me

the cat punches out a rickroll
the man skates into a piñata, his children
flying like wigged pins

all signs of the feeling, nothing escapes it
bodies whipping like hagfish in the sun

every cell of you is precious
like an Alcatraz full of wholesome celebrities

what else is there to say? to err is human, to forgive divine –
but loving you
is peanut butter jelly time

PART 2.

Stop Kicking

stop kicking   the back of my chair   aditya chanrai
     it's not my fault   they call you   chunky
booger goblin   fat spice   not your fault
     they call me   dick fetus   lord queerington III
"the smell"   you don't   need   to kick my chair
     aditya   I'm kicking it myself   galloping
toward revenge   in the form of a poem   I'll write
     years from now   a poem that reveals
the embarrassing birthmark   on your ass
     (I told everyone)   & you couldn't kick
a ball for shit   just like me   & just like you
     I kicked   adam dangoor's chair   & adam
kicked will morland's chair   & will kicked curran
     vedi's chair   & curran kicked your chair   & you
kicked your own chair   out   beneath   your legs
     dangled   like a big spider   kicking   I heard
in class   raspberry walls   stop it aditya
     it isn't funny   I'm not turning around

To Argue With the Person You Love

it's like vomiting diamonds, with which to buy your own silence
you scream and scream and nothing comes out but children

it's a lizard whose tongue is an identical smaller lizard
it's the tantalising shake of an envelope full of rage dollars

it's two lip-covered claws locked in an intimate arm wrestle
it's the bidets of the mind colliding with the urinals of the soul

it's a spicy flambé of hanging on to a point that has already receded
so far into memory that its only hope of persisting as a recalled mental event

lies in your clinging to it grimly, with steel chef's tongs
it's a delicious form of *ressentiment*, a hot fondue with bonus shrapnel

it's the futile application of poisoned lipstick to a pig
it's turning the other cheek en route to a roundhouse kick

it's a film treatment for the Holy Bible written from the perspective of a sandal
it's disappearing into the divorce, like a tsar with embezzled funds

you swore you'd be different, you swore and you swore and you swore
it's Barbie kicking ten kinds of shit out of Spiderman

Martial Arts Class, Aged 14

AGAIN cries dojo Morpheus as we rattle through the scales
of our karate symphony / punch scherzo / nocturne of "hwuh".
Neo and Trinity are my pet names for my hypertrophied triceps
but between friends we refer to them as Triceratops 1 / 2.
Between bouts Morpheus' head is a shining mosquito bulb;
I billow up tasty smoke meringue from an ever-present cigarillo.
We've been fighting in this theoretical room for theoretical hours.
I don't have big arms / We can't speak through our fists.
I'm so terribly bored with life / This never happened.

How Clumsy of You

You make me sad. So sad
I stare out the window etc. Outside, the suicide rate
soars romantically. Lovers softening
in baths of soil. What an eyesore.
Excuse me, I'm weeping.
I've squandered my hotness capital, that's clear enough –
and you won't even sing the Marseillaise!
And you've stepped on all my cakes again.
Resentment runs down my cheeks
in two clear plastic stretch limousines.
I thought we were living in a romantic French film –
turns out it was just Canadian.
I thought we were living
in a Richard Curtis rom com, but now things have become
irreversibly European.
I was watching Troy (2004) the other day; that Greek air
of lofty resignation really speaks to me.
I wondered why the things we love most easily
are the defenceless, exhausted things.
Ducklings, persimmons. The radical left. I could spend hours admiring
Brad Pitt's perfect pecs,
but could I ever truly love them?
Could I ever feel truly seen by them?
Lately even the bin bags regard me with sympathy
as they're flung onto steel compactors and crushed.
How careless of you.
How clumsy of you.
You keep forgetting to throw me out

THE RYAN POEM

The sky's good intentions fracture
into liquid pearls as I consider the famous Ryan
whose hips I want to wear as a leg napkin.

I consider this Ryan, consider him wrapped
around me like celebrity vacuum cleaner,
hoovering the arousal right out my mouth.

But then my brain conjures a different Ryan –
not Gosling or Reynolds: a glorious in-between.
A Ryan for whom I'd felt something like love,

lying on the cold diamond shingle of Depression Island.
My therapist at that time was also called Ryan;
he wanted me to live on a yoga mat forever,

palms like two warm sirloins cooking on my eyes.
My inner Ryan would shout at me to do something,
but I didn't know what that something was.

I suppose that was anxiety, in a nutshell that was it.
My therapist would remind me that routine is important:
we eat and sleep out of habit more than duty,

but you can't always trust habit now can you Ryan.
Like one time I watched your very special hands
put all the things they'd touched in a tidy little box,

then the slow click of the door on its latch.
I lay with my head under the duvet, my face sticky,
somebody spoke to me, then, a small voice I'd ignored a long time.

It was the poet Kay Ryan, reminding me that
sometimes *the green pasture of the mind tilts abruptly*.
It was Kay Ryan offering me the *greenest saddest strongest kind of hope*.

In the end, though I'm no movie star, I am also a little attractive.
In my own modest way this will always be true.
There's really no need to look for Ryanhood in another.

I look out of the window at the rain playing eternal chopsticks
thinking about this Ryan and that, and the one after that,
and the one after.

Feel the name in my mouth like a ragged bell,
inside me something is shimmering:
pool of night, gown of stars.

THE DEVIL

      it's okay to wish yourself dead
                at sixteen

admiring your reflection in a black spoon

       ~

        the face
pocked
     scrunched

a pomegranate whose seeds are falling

       ~

acres of pain crawl through the holes
             between stars

you have zero desire to achieve things

       ~

in fact
you have the opposite of that desire

       ~

sitting in the shower,
     dissolving in a water sonata

           experiencing
a hot flush burn like shame
         at wishing

     yourself, like, totally gone

       ~

preserved potential
in a depressurised tank full of yellow bats

        a dark, scrunched
pomegranate whose seeds are falling out

FOR MY 11TH BIRTHDAY

My parents bought me a Ninja Turtle miscoloured in shocking blue, and I cried as if they'd crushed my fingers in a car door. *You fucking wizards! How did you know?* I screamed in my child-voice as the guilt of having a nice thing cawed from its raggedy nest in my head. In retrospect, it was a strange thing to get so worked up about. By temperament or physical law I was destined to be of purest Goth, but there lurked in me an embarrassing zestiness and attraction to kitsch: plastic flamingos, tea cosies, Leslie Nielsen. A pink glow throbbed at the centre of my bitter façade, so like a perfumed vampire I would waft unmenacingly through the whole tint of adolescence, inconsolably happy. My parents told me off for swearing and bought me ice cream; I held the little blue homunculus and felt myself the envy of the civilised world. I even took it into the latrine, clutched it to my chest as the adults poured liquid stink around me – I didn't even care. Yellow milk caught on the turtle's brow and lit its frown with holy flame. When I lost the doll I cried and was comforted, and the feeling stuck with me ever after, like honey on a napkin.

Absolute Radiance

i beat ascended absolute radiance in hollow knight finally
only the top 2% of hollow knight players have done this
if i was in the top 2% of poets i might make a below-average uk salary
oh stop being such a hopeless romantic

i jump at the radiance and hit her twice with my nail
i hit her two more times before she teleports away
she shoots horizontal swords at me i dash between them
she spawns sun orbs i guide them harmlessly into the stage
why is life so endlessly disappointing and difficult?

the radiance is a grey moth who's infected the world with dream madness
i'm fighting her in the dream of my ancient bug predecessor, who locked
    her in his mind
now she's summoning the floor spikes, christ
i use the descending dark invincibility frames and get two more hits in
behind us the dream-space twinkles a creamy orange
there's a gap in life you could go mad trying to fill it

i hop from stage to stage dodging flying lasers
when they hit me black tendrils erupt from my little bug body
i can take three hits before experiencing frustration and death
until then i have a frantic life of dodging and hacking
this is the equilibrium we must spend ourselves to sustain

i warp dodge through a beam wall and double jump to safety
i pogo on the moth's wing, white flashes as each strike connects
as i make the final hit i feel a feeling
just before the 10 seconds of triumphant joy at completing an almost
    impossible task

the feeling is great anticipation that i am about to feel my 10 seconds
    of triumph
at the same time i feel sad that after those 10 seconds i will return
    to myself
i sit there with shaky hands waiting for my 10 seconds and wondering
what there is to do in life, and what have we done with all this time
and what is there to do in life
and then i feel the 10 seconds

PART 3.

WHITE CARNATIONS

The sun passes, dragging reluctant clouds
into the night. Glinting stars, spider's eggs.
We'll chat when you're home, my promise.
I lounge furtively in red trousers, needles
in my mouth. Old you, faux artiste. Just smile.
Every time I make some money I think *aha,*
now, now, now. Bricks block out the sunshine.
Like a baby ocean, I sometimes seem to be raging
but all I feel is the steady pull of the moon.
Everything a tiny piece of God, a body forever
ripping and sewing itself together, with a sort of
killer clown delight. What to do with winter.
No-one wants it, no-one can give it away.
Everyone's trying to starve it to death,
& sometimes it seems to: pale and translucent
as an empty bottle – but we find scraps, don't we?
Even during joy, which is irony's drought.
In times of happiness, a rustling in my ear, *the ripeness*
of the apple is its downfall etc. I've done my best
to stay green and watch the swans as if they were white
carnations, as if a white carnation was a solution
to the puzzle of flowers. Delight is a low bar,
only life above the planets is rich. See: Nutella.

BIRTH

Being born = one person coming out of another.
Apple trees weeping oranges.

I was born, screamed violet hell.
Thought I'd start as I meant to go on.

Cliff-diving into a dish of sea anemones.
Watching the anemones open and close
until a single sodden bee crawls out.

Some things get born. It'd be better if they didn't.
Not people. The things between them.

This one seemed to love it. Enough please, I said –
but life finds a way. To quote Jeff Goldblum.

Rescuing a fish from the ocean.
Removing a cucumber from a hot fridge.

Someone gave birth to some love, pushed it towards me.
Can't give birth myself, so I didn't return it.

I wanted to and then I didn't.
That should be easy to understand, but it isn't.

Some things are born from necessity.

Weaving a wig from your own thinning hair.
The world's first sentient guava juice.

Someone needed to bear that love,
if it was pushed towards me.

Maybe it was meant for someone other than me,
someone anatomically similar to me at that time
but *is* and *is like* are very different, I seem to recall.

E.g.:
being born *is like* cracking an egg into a waffle toaster,
but it's just a doll with another doll inside it.

Once, someone gave birth to someone else
and put me inside them. But the person I was inside
couldn't seem to learn even the basics of loving.

Like a balloon with a face painted on,
I thought I was one thing, then turned out to be another.

My pot plants flowered. Sun folded into the leaves
of the tulip buds. The purple hyacinth's silly loops
were like broken trumpets, flaring against spring.

THE FUTURE IS A GIFT HORSE

whose mouth we must look into all our lives.
I can never remember what kismet means

but that's what I've decided
to name the horse.

~

december 13th - though it was daytime, a star fell.
it danced along the tips of the trees, glowing blue

then it jumped in my mouth, crawled down my throat
and ate my heart.

~

we crushed the horse bones down to powder,
sealed the powder in tiny capsules.

the capsules were the only way to leave the horse's body.
stepping outside, the city in flames.

~

fishing boats on a swirling lick of water.
a bright room where everyone wanted you to live.

crammed to the tits with sympathy I swear
I felt terribly guilty.

~

june 4th - rode along the beach,
spotted a face of chalk, beast of holes.

crown me with roses said the man
who had crawled to shore just to be born.

I hailed the chalk: ahoy

~

a horse, a man and a flame walk into
the ocean

find a bad thing so beautiful
that now it's a good thing.

   ~

the sea turns out to be a lake, the beach an island.
together they write the letter O

as in   O god
didn't we pass this way before

Ekphrastic Surrender Dream

In the photograph, a man in a white t-shirt runs his pinkie along his eyebrow. Long hair floats across his face like the tendrils of a jellyfish. Cords trail from ears to mouth to phone to floating cassette. The cassette player is silhouetted against the amber glow of the curtains. The man is singer for a band whose expression of raw naïve feeling is something I always denied myself, despite many efforts to stop. Self-denial became an addiction, and the addiction proved unbreakable, eventually coming to function as bedrock for a whole personality. Behind the man a hump of duvet crouches like a large and sinister mollusc. As if in triptych with the man are two gold statuettes on a shelf. The man is trying to look at himself but there is no mirror. He kneels with the cords in his mouth and gazes into his phone screen as if in prayer. The ribbing of his jeans ripples in the light; sand dunes patterned by wind. The shadowed loops of the mouth-held cord cross under each eye via the bridge of the nose in two elegant wings. The flat touch of his thumb on the phone screen throws the surrounding objects into a dark tableau vivant. At a party he once described me almost deformedly feminine in both appearance and temperament, and the idea stuck with me because even though I didn't believe in its literal truth, I did believe in the thought's power over me, and found myself surrendering to a role in life that I don't feel I ever consciously desired. The flat touch of the man's thumb promises not the replacement of ordinary life but its inversion, every atom charged and full of submarine purpose. It casts cruel thought-ripples and chokes the bubble of air of which each person is preciously a cage. Chokes it up to emerge and float and become one with a great transparency. I place my fingers on and around the photo and part the plastic. The man's voice fills the room and soon I have completely disappeared.

THE VISITORS

when they landed I was in my studio watching the air wriggle
like a belly dancer over the electric stove
I turned to my long-term live-in partner and said leave the TV on
we were naked and true to form
some were abducting politicians and disintegrating police officers
but most just wanted to meet the celebrities and buy designer clothes
I was especially disgusted at the ones who came to see me thinking
     I'd be interested
in their fawning imitations of my early work
have you considered genre fiction I asked mockingly
holding a review copy over my genitals and shielding my partner from sight
but it was also a long time since I'd spoken to anyone
truly sympathetic to my aesthetic sensibilities
they wore backwards baseball caps with antennae poking out the front
they loved the music of early Springsteen and late Debussy
they were generally unimpressed by western philosophy post-Oprah
but took Jaden Smith perplexingly seriously
they loathed Tarantino except Kill Bill Part 2, which they loved
sometimes they were hard to understand but we hammered out an agreement
when they left I looked at the stars and sighed
my eggs were ash in the pan and there was no sense in any of it

High-Concept Loafers

i.

A golden brick hammers the blue skull of the earth. It tips the earth
on its side to drink its oceans and I am dating someone and my friend
is dating someone too. We danced around each other for years
and now the dance is paused or finished and it's a relief not to wear
a horned mask with red mouth stuffed full of pineapple seeds.

ii.

Beautiful swirls in the wooden desk. There is specifically a swirl like an ear
I like to whisper to. Mating eels among the tangled cables. I am so hungry
I could eat this pen, black marrow. Ink elevator churning out letters.

iii.

I am hungry and wearing high-concept loafers. This is an affectation.
We do not speak of loafers here, because here there are no words,
just the silence of the Lamborghinis gliding icily overhead.

iv.

To wordlessly roam around a dead civilisation murdering giant salamanders
is what I plan to do when I finish this sandwich.

PERCOCET

this is for you in the future
where I'm buying you a post-watermelon watermelon: it's a cucumber

you're warning me about the chef who rules the sky
and sure enough, combat music erupts when we meet

but don't worry, you say, it hasn't happened yet
besides, we may come to love that chef

when we say grace, we armwrestle at the same time
thank you invisibility lotion, thank you ugly lovers

I doff my hat to the dying embers of civilisation
hat-doffing being briefly back in fashion

you chew dutifully on the cud of each day
searching for a final flavour to go out on

but no-one likes a try-hard, Charlie, nobody

you say you don't regret being a Smiths fan
I say I don't regret meeting you

and as the ice caps rain we drink Percocet

A List of Fantastical Objects

it's never been my ambition to compile one   *earl grey*
jacuzzi   *violin defoliant*   never anyone's perhaps
but here we are   *burlap nightingale*   *crustacean paraglider*
abandoning the mundane, taking it off like an austerity cravat
spicy ricochet   it's never been my ambition to serve
a three-thousand course meal   of charcuterie errata
scarlet gramophone   *regret piñata*   unless every course
is just a different flavour   of exhausting wisecrack
tulip razor   *war yoghurt*   at least my writer friends
can laugh over this   before submitting it once again
to their strict standards   of relevance and specificity
emotional honesty   acoustic structure   *swole banana*
but looking back   at a hundred years of realist production
I find it all deeply suspect   *masculine pedantry*
like an angularly handsome hotel lasagne   *chardonnay*
pyjamas   *goblin carafe*   as if a metaphysical cabal
had taken reality hostage   *umbrellas akimbo*   for a massive
attention ransom   *revenge salmon*   but if you want
a startling description   of a sunset   *the very notion*
of a literary canon   go look at a sunset   ...
...   ...   *jamiroquai*

THE MEANING IS THERE

They say the meaning is right there in the words but I feel it
in the billion minds riding the WiFi air
in the paradigm-shattering historic world event
in the intricate sexuality of class politics
in the forbidden lyric impulse
everything is becoming passé and it has frightened the adults
but only when Spike is beyond memory will I have truly died
I reach for a glass of water but the taps only dispense vampire juice
I reach for my glasses of water but can only wear them when I'm feeling sad
everything has become complex and strange, I feel it in my hind-brain
in the leaf blower's gusting footsteps
in the convertible's sub-bass manifesto
I am trying to write a poem
about a feeling too stupid for poetry
I am searching for a poem about a feeling that I am too stupid to understand
but I feel it
in the collective hysteria of potted plants
when you rigorously interpret me 'for my own good'
when you insightfully perceive me against the court's order
in the zirconian bevels of your oopsing eyes
sometimes things get dangerously *à la carte*
and that's when the bigwigs step in, dripping small change from their noses
in some cultures it is cool to eat bugs, or buy a car instead of world peace
but going crazy is ultimately a waste of inspiration
sometimes life gets pretty decent
and we're allowed to sink, finally
into the deep pastas of online entertainment
some things are as hard to live with as without
a lover is one of those things, and another is expecting things of yourself
you can get wise or you can get bitter
if I were a tree I would go to Homebase and gloat at the soil bags
cut to Homer scratching his chin and saying

> The End
>
> or is it?

NOTES

"Crown me with roses" – is a Pessoa poem

"the ripeness of the apple is its downfall" – is from "The Orchard" by Mary Oliver

"Good heavens… I'm just like a pile of leaves" – is from "Meditations in an Emergency" by Frank O'Hara

"what is a man, a miserable pile of secrets" – is from Castlevania: Symphony of the Night. Original quote: *Pour l'essentiel, l'homme est ce qu'il cache : un misérable petit tas de secrets* - André Malraux

"I rebelled in silent ways, with my thoughts" – is from *My Year of Rest and Relaxation* by Ottessa Moshfegh

"Don't. Make. People." – is from Brad Neely's "The Future"

"moonbeams kiss the sea" – is from "Love's Philosophy" by Percy Shelley

"at every pore with instant fires" – is from "To His Coy Mistress" by Andrew Marvell

"Sometimes the green pasture of the mind tilts abruptly" – is from "Grazing Horses" by Kay Ryan

"greenest saddest strongest kind of hope" – is from "A Certain Kind of Eden" by Kay Ryan

"O, no! Alas, I rather hate myself…" – is from Richard III

"you make me sad, so sad I stare out the window etc." – is from *Poemland* by Chelsey Minnis

About the Author

OLIVER SEDANO-JONES is a British-Peruvian writer. His work is published in *Banshee*, *Tears in the Fence*, *Ink Sweat and Tears*, *SPOONFEED* and *Prototype*. Oliver was shortlisted for the Yeats Prize in 2018, the University of Hertfordshire Single Poem Prize in 2019 and the Wales Poetry Award 2020.

If You Like Oliver Sedano-Jones, Oliver Likes...

Hard Summer
Francisca Matos

Ping!
Iain Whiteley

What We Are Given
Ollie O' Neill

Bloody beautiful poetry books.

Write Bloody UK is an independent poetry publisher passionate
about bringing the voices of UK poets to the masses.
Trailing after Write Bloody Publishing (US) and
Write Bloody North (Canada), we are committed to
handling the creation, distribution and marketing of our authors;
binding their words in beautiful, velvety-to-the-touch books
and touring loudly with them through UK cities.

Support independent authors, artists, and presses.

Want to know more about Write Bloody UK books, authors, and events?
Join our mailing list at

www.writebloodyuk.co.uk

WRITE BLOODY UK BOOKS

Lightning Source UK Ltd.
Milton Keynes UK
UKHW011810250223
417652UK00002B/5

9 781838 033248